MW00768118

friendship

friendship

Great Minds on
the Deepest Bond

To my Dear Friend Sue
Christmas 1999
Love, Judi

EDITED BY JOHN MILLER AND AARON KENEDI

WILLIAM MORROW AND COMPANY, INC.

NEW YORK

It is the policy of William Morrow and Company, Inc., and its imprints and
affiliates, recognizing the importance of preserving what has been written, to print
the books we publish on acid-free paper, and we exert our best efforts to that end.

Library of Congress Cataloging-in-Publication Data
Friendship : great minds on the deepest bond /
edited by John Miller and Aaron Kenedi.
p.   cm.
ISBN: 0-688-17273-3
1. Friendship—Anecdotes.   I. Miller, John, 1959—
II. Kenedi, Aaron.
BF575.F66F73   1999
808.8'0353—dc21   99-41557
CIP

Printed in the United States of America
First Edition
1 2 3 4 5 6 7 8 9 10
www.williammorrow.com

SPECIAL THANKS TO:

KIM INDRESANO

BESSIE WEISS

ELEANOR REAGH

AMY RENNERT

contents

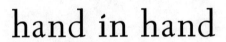

hand in hand

"What is a friend? A single soul in two bodies."

—ARISTOTLE

Rosie

ANNE LAMOTT

Rosie and Sharon walked into town to buy M&M's with their allowances, then walked to their newest fort, the basement of the old Murphy house, which had gone unsold since the midnight a year ago when Mrs. Murphy passed out smoking in bed. No one had locked the door to the now empty basement, a low dark room that was dank and dusty at the same time; the floor was dirt and the rafters were filled with cobwebs and spiders.

They ate their M&M's one at a time, savoring them, sucking through the thin sugar crust into the melting chocolate, proclaiming the red ones the best, the green ones a close second, the orange ones almost inedible. When the candies were gone, they spent a few minutes turning their eyelids inside out. And then they took turns helping each other pass out.

Long ago they had discovered the wonders of dizziness, the altered state that could be achieved by winding up a rope swing tightly and unspinning at a wild, exhilarating pace, the pleasure of giddy confusion, of staggering around drunkenly until their heads cleared. But passing out for the weirdness of the coming-to was much more scary and fun.

As usual, Rosie went first. She hyperventilated until she was woozy, then nodded to Sharon and lifted her arms so that Sharon could give her one hard, quick squeeze in the stomach from behind. Rosie crumpled onto the soft dirt, out for seconds, then began spinning back to earth through a long tunnel of whirling colors—feather-headed, intoxicated, out of her mind, blissfully confused. As she opened her eyes, a vision of Sharon swam before her, but gradually the distortion slowed down, like the end of a carousel ride. Sharon's image was clear as a bell, and Rosie was smiling drunkenly.

Sharon set her broad jaw into a grimace and began the staccato breathing, scared to death; she nodded, was squeezed, and passed out, began the long swim through the tunnel back to earth, high as a kite. Rosie panicked each time Sharon crumpled to the ground—no sign of life, she was dead, she was dead—and hardly breathed until Sharon opened her unfocusing eyes with a faraway smile.

The third-grader who had taught them how to do this had told them that each time you did it, billions of brain cells were killed, but they did it over and over again anyway.

Bulletproof Diva

LISA JONES

Donna and Lorna together. Friends for ages from Queens who found their way to the Rodeo. Their sign language is all raised eyebrows and pursed lips. They converse in an intricate syncretic dialect of Queens b-girl, art criticism, and haute couture-speak known only to sets of Silent Twins. Them giggling and leaning against each other expresses all that I love about being a colored girl. They are always in conspiracy; a whisper, a poke, then Lorna's belly laugh and Donna's tee-hees. Lorna's skin is seamless brown silk, Donna's all cream. Their difference in color is minus the familiar divide of privilege and shame and seems to exist just for our looking pleasure. They must know how beautiful they are side by side; they cannot contain their good fortune to be, as Nel longs for Sula, girls together. Thick as thieves, rushing boys' hearts with a glance. If we all could be like Donna and Lorna, girls together.

A Separate Peace

JOHN KNOWLES

I went back to the Devon School not long ago, and found it looking oddly newer than when I was a student there fifteen years before. It seemed more sedate than I remembered it, more perpendicular and strait-laced, with narrower windows and shinier woodwork, as though a coat of varnish had been put over everything for better preservation. But, of course, fifteen years before there had been a war going on. Perhaps the school wasn't as well kept up in those days; perhaps varnish, along with everything else, had gone to war.

I started the long trudge across the fields and had gone some distance before I paid any attention to the soft and muddy ground, which was dooming my city shoes. I didn't stop. Near the center of the fields there were thin lakes of muddy water which I had to make my way around, my unrecognizable shoes making obscene noises as I lifted them out of the mire. With nothing to block it the wind flung wet gusts at me; at any other time I would have felt like a fool slogging through mud and rain, only to look at a tree.

A little fog hung over the river so that as I neared it I felt myself becoming isolated from everything except the river and the few trees beside it. The wind was blowing more steadily here, and I was beginning to feel cold. I never wore a hat, and had forgotten gloves. There were several trees bleakly reaching into the fog. Any one of them might have been the one I was looking for. Unbelievable that there were other trees which looked like it here. It had loomed in my memory as a huge lone spike dominating the riverbank forbidding as an artillery piece, high as the beanstalk. Yet here was a scattered grove of trees, none of them of any particular grandeur.

Moving through the soaked, coarse grass I began to examine each one closely, and finally identified the tree I was looking for by means of certain small scars rising along its trunk, and by a limb extending over the river, and another thinner limb growing near it. This was the tree, and it seemed to me standing there to resemble those men, the giants of your childhood, whom you encounter years later and find that they are not merely smaller in relation to your growth, but that they are absolutely smaller, shrunken by age. In this double demotion the old giants have become pygmies while you were looking the other way.

The tree was not only stripped by the cold season, it seemed weary from age, enfeebled, dry. I was thankful, very thankful that I had seen it. So the more things remain the same, the more they change after all —*plus c'est la même chose, plus ça change.* Nothing endures, not a tree, not love, not even a death by violence.

Changed, I headed back through the mud. I was drenched; anybody could see it was time to come in out of the rain.

The tree was tremendous, an irate, steely black steeple beside the river. I was damned if I'd climb it. The hell with it. No one but Phineas could think up such a crazy idea.

He of course saw nothing the slightest bit intimidating about it. He wouldn't, or wouldn't admit it if he did. Not Phineas.

"What I like best about this tree," he said in that voice of his, the equivalent in sound of a hypnotist's eyes, "what I like is that it's such a cinch!" He opened his green eyes wider and gave us his maniac look, and only the smirk on his wide mouth with its droll, slightly protruding upper lip reassured us that he wasn't completely goofy.

"Is that what you like best?" I said sarcastically. I said a lot of things sarcastically that summer; that was my sarcastic summer, 1942.

"Aey-uh," he said. This weird New England affirmative—maybe it is spelled "aie-huh"—always made me laugh, as Finny knew, so I had to laugh, which made me feel less sarcastic and less scared.

There were three others with us—Phineas in those days almost always moved in groups the size of a hockey team—and they stood with me looking with masked apprehension from him to the tree. Its soaring black trunk was set with rough wooden pegs leading up to a substantial limb which extended farther toward the water. Standing on this limb, you could by a prodigious effort jump far enough out into the river for safety. So we had heard. At least the seventeen-year-old bunch could do it; but they had a crucial year's advantage over us. No Upper Middler, which was the name for our class in the Devon School, had ever tried. Naturally Finny was going to be the first to try, and just as naturally he was going to inveigle others, us, into trying it with him.

We were not even Upper Middler exactly. For this was the

Summer Session, just established to keep up with the pace of the war. We were in shaky transit that summer from the groveling status of Lower Middlers to the near-respectability of Upper Middlers. The class above, seniors, draft-bait, practically soldiers, rushed ahead of us toward the war. They were caught up in accelerated courses and first-aid programs and a physical hardening regimen, which included jumping from this tree. We were still calmly, numbly reading Virgil and playing tag in the river farther downstream. Until Finny thought of the tree.

We stood looking up at it, four looks of consternation, one of excitement. "Do you want to go first?" Finny asked us, rhetorically. We just looked quietly back at him, and so he began taking off his clothes, stripping down to his underpants. For such an extraordinary athlete—even as a Lower Middler Phineas had been the best athlete in the school—he was not spectacularly built. He was my height—five feet eight and a half inches (I had been claiming five feet nine inches before he became my roommate, but he had said in public with that simple, shocking self-acceptance of his, "No, you're the same height I am, five eight and a half. We're on the short side"). He weighed a hundred and fifty pounds, a galling ten pounds more than I did, which flowed from his legs to torso around shoulders to arms and full strong neck in an uninterrupted, unemphatic unity of strength.

He began scrambling up the wooden pegs nailed to the side of the tree, his back muscles working like a panther's. The pegs didn't seem strong enough to hold his weight. At last he stepped onto the branch which reached a little farther toward the water. "Is this the one they jump from?" None of us knew. "If I do it, you're all going to do it, aren't you?" We didn't say anything very clearly; "Well," he cried out, "here's my contribution to the war effort!" and he sprang out, fell through the tops of some lower branches, and smashed into the water.

"Great!" he said, bobbing instantly to the surface again, his wet hair plastered in droll bangs on his forehead. "That's the most fun I've had this week. Who's next?"

I was. This tree flooded me with a sensation of alarm all the way to my tingling fingers. My head began to feel unnaturally light, and the vague rustling sounds from the nearby woods came to me as though muffled and filtered. I must have been entering a mild state of shock. Insulated by this, I took off my clothes and started to climb the pegs. I don't remember saying anything. The branch he had jumped from was slenderer than it looked from the ground and much higher. It was impossible to walk out on it far enough to be well over the river. I would have to spring far out or risk falling into the shallow water next to the bank. "Come on," drawled Finny from below, "stop standing there showing off." I recognized with automatic tenseness that the view was very impressive from here. "When they torpedo the troopship," he shouted, "you can't stand around admiring the view. Jump!"

What was I doing up here anyway? Why did I let Finny talk me into stupid things like this? Was he getting some kind of hold over me?

"Jump!"

With the sensation that I was throwing my life away, I jumped into space. Some tips of branches snapped past me and then I crashed into the water. My legs hit the soft mud of the bottom, and immediately I was on the surface being congratulated. I felt fine.

"I think that was better than Finny's," said Elwin—better known as Leper—Lepellier, who was bidding for an ally in the dispute he foresaw.

"All right, pal," Finny spoke in his cordial, penetrating voice, that reverberant instrument in his chest, "don't start awarding prizes until you've passed the course. The tree is waiting."

Leper closed his mouth as though forever. He didn't argue or refuse. He didn't back away. He became inanimate. But the other two, Chet Douglass and Bobby Zane, were vocal enough, complaining shrilly about school regulations, the danger of stomach cramps; physical disabilities they had never mentioned before.

"It's you, pal," Finny said to me at last, "just you and me." He and I started back across the fields, preceding the others like two seigneurs.

We were the best of friends at that moment.

"You were very good," said Finny good-humoredly, "once I shamed you into it."

"You didn't shame anybody into anything."

"Oh yes I did. I'm good for you that way. You have a tendency to back away from things otherwise."

"I never backed away from anything in my life!" I cried, my indignation at this charge naturally stronger because it was so true. "You're goofy!"

Phineas just walked serenely on, or rather flowed on, rolling forward in his white sneakers with such unthinking unity of movement that "walk" didn't describe it.

I went along beside him across the enormous playing fields toward the gym. Underfoot the healthy green turf was brushed with dew, and ahead of us we could see a faint green haze hanging above the grass, shot through with the twilight sun. Phineas stopped talking for once, so that now I could hear cricket noises and bird cries of dusk, a gymnasium truck gunning along an empty athletic road a quarter of a mile away, a burst of faint, isolated laughter carried to us from the back door of the gym, and then over all, cool and matriarchal, the six o'clock bell from the Academy Building cupola, the calmest, most carrying bell toll in the world, civilized, calm, invincible, and final.

The toll sailed over the expansive tops of all the elms, the great slanting roofs and formidable chimneys of the dormitories, the narrow and brittle old housetops, across the open New Hampshire sky to us coming back from the river. "We'd better hurry or we'll be late for dinner," I said, breaking into what Finny called my "West Point stride." Phineas didn't really dislike West Point in particular or authority in general, but just considered authority the necessary evil against which happiness was achieved by reaction, the backboard which returned all the insults he threw at it. My "West Point stride" was intolerable; his right foot flashed into the middle of my fast walk and I went pitching forward into the grass. "Get those hundred and fifty pounds off me!" I shouted, because he was sitting on my back. Finny got up, patted my head genially, and moved on across the field, not deigning to glance around for my counterattack but relying on his extrasensory ears, his ability to feel in the air someone coming on him from behind. As I sprang at him he side-stepped easily, but I just managed to kick him as I shot past. He caught my leg and there was a brief wrestling match on the turf which he won. "Better hurry," he said, "or they'll put you in the guardhouse." We were walking again, faster; Bobby and Leper and Chet were urging us from ahead for God's sake to hurry up, and then Finny trapped me again in his strongest trap, that is, I suddenly became his collaborator. As we walked rapidly along I abruptly resented the bell and my West Point stride and hurrying and conforming. Finny was right. And there was only one way to show him this. I threw my hip against his, catching him by surprise, and he was instantly down, definitely pleased. This was why he liked me so much. When I jumped on top of him, my knees on his chest, he couldn't ask for anything better. We struggled in some equality for a while, and then when we were sure we were too late for dinner, we broke off.

He and I passed the gym and came on toward the first group of dormitories, which were dark and silent. There were only two hundred of us at Devon in the summer, not enough to fill most of the school. We passed the sprawling Headmaster's house—empty, he was doing something for the government in Washington; past the Chapel—empty again, used only for a short time in the mornings; past the First Academy Building, where there were some dim lights shining from a few of its many windows, Masters at work in their classrooms there; down a short slope into the broad and well clipped Common, on which light fell from the big surrounding Georgian buildings. A dozen boys were loafing there on the grass after dinner, and a kitchen rattle from the wing of one of the buildings accompanied their talk. The sky was darkening steadily, which brought up the lights in the dormitories and the old houses; a loud phonograph a long way off played *Don't Sit Under the*

Apple Tree, rejected that and played *They're Either Too Young or Too Old*, grew more ambitious with *The Warsaw Concerto*, mellower with *The Nutcracker Suite*, and then stopped.

Finny and I went to our room. Under the yellow study lights we read our Hardy assignments; I was halfway through *Tess of the D'Urbervilles*, he carried on his baffled struggle with *Far from the Madding Crowd*, amused that there should be people named Gabriel Oak and Bathsheba Everdene. Our illegal radio, tuned too low to be intelligible, was broadcasting the news. Outside there was a rustling early summer movement of the wind; the seniors, allowed out later than we were, came fairly quietly back as the bell sounded ten stately times. Boys ambled past our door toward the bathroom, and there was a period of steadily pouring shower water. Then lights began to snap out all over the school. We undressed, and I put on some pajamas, but Phineas, who had heard they were unmilitary, didn't; there was the silence in which it was understood we were saying some prayers, and then that summer school day came to an end.

Fried Green Tomatoes

FANNIE FLAGG

Ruth had been in Whistle Stop for about two months, and this Saturday morning, someone knocked at her bedroom window at 6 A.M. Ruth opened her eyes and saw Idgie sitting in the chinaberry tree and motioning for her to open the window.

Ruth got up, half asleep. "What are you up so early for?"

"You promised we could go on a picnic today."

"I know, but does it have to be this early? It's Saturday."

"Please. You promised you would. If you don't come right now, I'll jump off the roof and kill myself. Then what would you do?"

Ruth laughed. "Well, what about Patsy Ruth and Mildred and Essie Rue, aren't they going to come with us?"

"No."

"Don't you think we should ask them?"

"No. Please, I want you to myself. Please. I want to show you something."

"Idgie, I don't want to hurt their feelings."

"Oh, you won't hurt their feelings. They don't want to come anyhow. I asked them already, and they want to stay home in case their old stupid boyfriends come by."

"Are you sure?"

"Sure I'm sure," she lied.

"What about Ninny and Julian?"

"They said they've got things to do today. Come on, Ruth, Sipsey's already made us a lunch, just for the two of us. If you don't come, I'll jump and then you'll have my death on your hands. I'll be dead in my grave and you'll wish you'd have come to just one little picnic."

"Well, all right. Let me get dressed, at least."

"Hurry up! Don't get all dressed up, just come on out—I'll meet you in the car."

"Are we going in the car?"

"Sure. Why not?"

"Okay."

Idgie had failed to mention that she had sneaked into Julian's room at 5 A.M. and had stolen the keys to his Model T out of his pants pockets, and it was extremely important to get going before he woke up.

They drove way out to this place that Idgie had found years ago, by Double Springs Lake, where there was a waterfall that flowed into this crystal clear stream that was filled with beautiful brown and gray stones, as round and smooth as eggs.

Idgie spread the blanket out and got the basket out of the car. She was being very mysterious.

Finally, she said, "Ruth, if I show you something, do you swear that you will never tell another living soul?"

"Show me what? What is it?"

"Do you swear? You won't tell?"

"I swear. What is it?"

"I'll show you."

Idgie reached into the picnic basket and got out an empty glass jar, said, "Let's go," and they walked about a mile back up into the woods.

Idgie pointed to a tree and said, "There it is!"

"There is what?"

"That big oak tree over there."

"Oh."

She took Ruth by the hand and walked her over to the left,

about one hundred feet away, behind a tree, and said, "Now, Ruth, you stay right here, and no matter what happens, don't move."

"What are you going to do?"

"Never mind, you just watch me, all right? And be quiet. Don't make any noise, whatever you do."

Idgie, who was barefoot, started walking over to the big oak tree and about halfway there, turned to see if Ruth was watching. When she got about ten feet from the tree, she made sure again that Ruth was still watching. Then she did the most amazing thing. She very slowly tiptoed up to it, humming very softly, and stuck her hand with the jar in it, right in the hole in the middle of the oak.

All of a sudden, Ruth heard a sound like a buzz saw, and the sky went black as hordes of angry bees swarmed out of the hole.

In seconds, Idgie was covered from head to foot with thousands of bees. Idgie just stood there, and in a minute, carefully pulled her hand out of the tree and started walking slowly back toward Ruth, still humming. By the time she had gotten back, almost all the bees had flown away and what had been a completely black figure was now Idgie, standing there, grinning from ear to ear, with a jar of wild honey.

She held it up, offering the jar to Ruth. "Here you are, madame, this is for you."

Ruth, who had been scared out of her wits, slid down the tree onto the ground, and burst into tears. "I thought you were dead! Why did you do that? You could have been killed!"

Idgie said, "Oh, don't cry. I'm sorry. Here, don't you want the honey? I got it just for you . . . please don't cry. It's all right, I do it all the time. I never get stung. Honest. Here, let me help you up, you're getting yourself all dirty."

She handed Ruth the old blue bandanna she had in her overalls pocket. Ruth was still shaky, but she got up and blew her nose and wiped off her dress.

Idgie tried to cheer her up. "Just think, Ruth, I never did it for anybody else before. Now nobody in the whole world knows I can do that but you. I just wanted for us to have a secret together, that's all."

Ruth didn't respond.

"I'm sorry, Ruth, please don't be mad at me."

"Mad?" Ruth put her arms around Idgie and said, "Oh

Idgie, I'm not mad at you. It's just that I don't know what I'd do if anything ever happened to you. I really don't."

Idgie's heart started pounding so hard it almost knocked her over.

After they had eaten the chicken and potato salad and all the biscuits and most of the honey, Ruth leaned back against the tree and Idgie put her head in her lap. "You know, Ruth, I'd kill for you. Anybody that would ever hurt you, I'd kill them in a minute and never think twice about it."

"Oh Idgie, that's a terrible thing to say."

"No it isn't. I'd rather kill for love than kill for hate. Wouldn't you?"

"Well, I don't think we should ever kill for any reason."

"All right, then, I'd die for you. How about that? Don't you think somebody could die for love?"

"No."

"The Bible says Jesus Christ did."

"That's different."

"No it isn't. I could die right now, and I wouldn't mind. I'd be the only corpse with a smile on my face."

"Don't be silly."

"I could have been killed today, couldn't I have?"

Ruth took her hand and smiled down at her. "My Idgie's a bee charmer."

"Is that what I am?"

"That's what you are. I've heard there were people who could do it, but I'd never seen one before today."

"Is it bad?"

"Nooo. It's wonderful. Don't you know that?"

"Naw, I thought it was crazy or something."

"No—it's a wonderful thing to be."

Ruth leaned down and whispered in her ear, "You're an old bee charmer, Idgie Threadgoode, that's what you are . . ."

Idgie smiled back at her and looked up into the clear blue sky that reflected in her eyes, and she was as happy as anybody who is in love in the summertime can be.

My Lucy Friend Who Smells Like Corn

SANDRA CISNEROS

Lucy Anguiano, Texas girl who smells like corn, like Frito Bandito chips, like tortillas, something like that warm smell of nixtamal or bread the way her head smells when she's leaning close to you over a paper cut-out doll or on the porch when we are squatting over marbles trading this pretty crystal that leaves a blue star on your hand for that giant cat-eye with a grasshopper green spiral in the center like the juice of bugs on the windshield when you drive to the border, like the yellow blood of butterflies.

Have you ever eated dog food? I have. After crunching like ice, she opens her big mouth to prove it, only a pink tongue rolling around in there like a blind worm, and Janey looking in because she said Show me. But me I like that Lucy, corn smell hair and aqua flip-flops just like mine that we bought at the K-mart for only 79 cents same time.

I'm going to sit in the sun, don't care if it's a million trillion degrees outside, so my skin can get so dark it's blue where it bends like Lucy's. Her whole family like that. Eyes like knife slits. Lucy and her sisters. Norma, Margarita, Ofelia, Herminia, Nancy, Olivia, Cheli, y la Amber Sue.

Screen door with no screen. Bang! Little black dog biting his fur. Fat couch on the porch. Some of the windows painted blue, some pink, because her daddy got tired that day or forgot. Mama in the kitchen feeding clothes into the wringer washer and clothes rolling out all stiff and twisted and flat like paper. Lucy got her arm stuck once and had to yell Maaa! and her mama had to put the machine in reverse and then her hand rolled back, the finger black and later, her nail fell off. *But did your arm get flat like the clothes? What happened to your arm? Did they have to pump it with air?* No, only the finger, and she didn't cry neither.

Lean across the porch rail and pin the pink sock of the baby Amber Sue on top of Cheli's flowered T-shirt, and the blue jeans of *la* Ofelia over the inside seam of Olivia's blouse, over the flannel nightgown of Margarita so it don't stretch out, and then you take the work shirts of their daddy and hang them upside down like this, and this way all the clothes don't get so wrinkled and take up less space and you don't waste pins. The girls all wear each other's clothes, except Olivia, who is stingy.

There ain't no boys here. Only girls and one father who is never home hardly and one mother who says *Ay! I'm real tired* and so many sisters there's no time to count them.

I'm sitting in the sun even though it's the hottest part of the day, the part that makes the streets dizzy, when the heat makes a little hat on the top of your head and bakes the dust and weed grass and sweat up good, all steamy and smelling like sweet corn.

I want to rub heads and sleep in bed with little sisters, some at the top and some at the feets. I think it would be fun to sleep with sisters you could yell at once at a time or all together, instead of alone on the fold-out chair in the living room.

When I get home Abuelita will say *Didn't I tell you?* and I'll get it because I was supposed to wear this dress again tomorrow. But first, I'm going to jump off an old pissy mattress in the Anguiano yard. I'm going to scratch your mosquito bites, Lucy, so they'll itch you, then put Mercurochrome smiley faces on them. We're going to trade shoes and wear them on our hands. We're going to walk over to Janey Ortiz's house and say We're never ever going to be your friend again forever! We're going to run home backwards and we're going to run home front-wards, look twice under the house where the rats hide and I'll stick one foot in there because you dared me, sky so blue and heaven inside those white clouds. I'm going to peel nine scab from my knee and eat it, sneeze on the cat, give you three M & M's I've been saving for you since yesterday, comb your hair with my fingers and braid it into teeny-tiny braids real pretty. We're going to wave to a lady we don't know on the bus. Hello! I'm going to somersault on the rail of the front porch even though my chones show. And cut paper dolls we draw ourselves, and color in their clothes with crayons, my arm around your neck.

And when we look at each other, our arms gummy from an orange Popsicle we split, we could be sisters, right? We could be, you and me waiting for our teeth to fall and money. You laughing something into my ear that tickles, and me going Ha Ha Ha Ha. Her and me, my Lucy friend who smells like corn.

true devotion

"The greatest love a person can have for his friends is to give his life for them."

–JESUS

For the Love of Man

JACK LONDON

When John Thornton froze his feet in the previous December, his partners had made him comfortable and left him to get well, going on themselves up the river to get out a raft of saw-logs for Dawson. He was still limping slightly at the time he rescued Buck, but with the continued warm weather even the slight limp left him. And here, lying by the river bank through the long spring days, watching the running water, listening lazily to the songs of birds and the hum of nature, Buck slowly won back his strength.

A rest comes very good after one has travelled three thousand miles, and it must be confessed that Buck waxed lazy as his wounds healed, his muscles swelled out, and the flesh came back to cover his bones. For that matter, they were all loafing—Buck, John Thornton, and Skeet and Nig— waiting for the raft to come that was to carry them down to Dawson. Skeet was a little Irish setter who early made friends with Buck, who, in a dying condition, was unable to resent her first advances. She had the doctor trait which some dogs possess, and as a mother cat washes her kittens, so she washed and cleansed Buck's wounds. Regularly, each morning after he had finished his breakfast, she performed her self-appointed task, till he came to look for her ministrations as much as he did for Thornton's. Nig, equally friendly, though less demonstrative, was a huge black dog, half bloodhound and half deerhound, with eyes that laughed and a boundless good nature.

To Buck's surprise these dogs manifested no jealousy toward him. They seemed to share the kindliness and largeness of John Thornton. As Buck grew stronger they enticed him into all sorts of ridiculous games, in which Thornton himself could not forbear to join, and in this fashion Buck romped through his convalescence and into a new existence. Love, genuine passionate love, was his for the first time. This he had never experienced at Judge Miller's down in the sunkissed Santa Clara Valley. With the Judge's sons, hunting and tramping, it had been a working partnership; with the Judge's grandsons, a sort of pompous guardianship; and with the Judge himself, a stately and dignified friendship. But love that was feverish and burning, that was adoration, that was madness, it had taken John Thornton to arouse.

This man had saved his life, which was something; but, further, he was the ideal master. Other men saw to the welfare of their dogs from a sense of duty and business expediency; he saw to the welfare of his as if they were his own children, because he could not help it. And he saw further. He never forgot a kindly greeting or a cheering word, and to sit down for a long talk with them ("gas" he called it) was as much his delight as theirs. He had a way of taking Buck's head roughly between his hands, and resting his own head upon Buck's, of shaking him back and forth, the while calling him ill names that to Buck were love names. Buck knew no greater joy than that rough embrace and the sound of murmured oaths, and at each jerk; back and forth it seemed that his heart would be shaken out of his body so great was his ecstasy. And when, released, he sprang to his feet, his mouth laughing, his eyes eloquent, his throat vibrant with unuttered sound, and in that fashion remained without movement, John Thornton would reverently exclaim, "God! you can all but speak!"

Buck had a trick of love expression that was akin to hurt.

He would often seize Thornton's hand in his mouth and close so fiercely that the flesh bore the impress of his teeth for some time afterward. And as Buck understood the oaths to be love words, so the man understood this feigned bite for a caress.

For the most part, however, Buck's love was expressed in adoration. While he went wild with happiness when Thornton touched him or spoke to him, he did not seek these tokens. Unlike Skeet, who was wont to shove her nose under Thornton's hand and nudge and nudge till petted, or Nig, who would stalk up and rest his great head on Thornton's knee, Buck was content to adore at a distance. He would lie by the hour, eager, alert, at Thornton's feet, looking up into his face, dwelling upon it, studying it, following with keenest interest each fleeting expression, every movement or change of feature. Or, as chance might have it, he would lie farther away, to the side or rear, watching the outlines of the man and the occasional movements of his body. And often, such was the communion in which they lived, the strength of Buck's gaze would draw John Thornton's head around, and he would return the gaze, without speech, his heart shining out of his eyes as Buck's heart shone out.

That winter, at Dawson, Buck performed another exploit. It was brought about by a conversation in the Eldorado Saloon, in which men waxed boastful of their favorite dogs. Buck, because of his record, was the target for these men, and Thornton was driven stoutly to defend him. At the end of half an hour one man stated that his dog could start a sled with five hundred pounds and walk off with it; a second bragged six hundred for his dog; and a third seven hundred.

"Pooh! pooh!" said John Thornton. "Buck can start a thousand pounds."

"And break it out? and walk off with it for a hundred yards?" demanded Matthewson, a Bonanza King, he of the seven hundred vaunt.

"And break it out, and walk off with it for a hundred yards," John Thornton said coolly.

"Well," Matthewson said, slowly and deliberately, so that all could hear, "I've got a thousand dollars that says he can't. And there it is." So saying, he slammed a sack of gold dust of the size of a bologna sausage down upon the bar.

Nobody spoke. Thornton's bluff, if bluff it was, had been called. He could feel a flush of warm blood creeping up his face.

His tongue had tricked him. He did not know whether Buck could start a thousand pounds. Half a ton! The enormousness of it appalled him. He had great faith in Buck's strength and had often thought him capable of starting such a load; but never, as now, had he faced the possibility of it, the eyes of a dozen men fixed upon him, silent and waiting. Further, he had no thousand dollars; nor had Hans or Pete.

"I've got a sled standing outside now, with twenty fifty-pound sacks of flour on it," Matthewson went on with brutal directness, "so don't let that hinder you."

Thornton did not reply. He did not know what to say. He glanced from face to face in the absent way of a man who has lost the power of thought and is seeking somewhere to find the thing that will start it going again. The face of Jim O'Brien, a Mastodon King and old-time comrade, caught his eyes. It was as a cue to him, seeming to rouse him to do what he would never have dreamed of doing.

"Can you lend me a thousand?" he asked, almost in a whisper.

"Sure," answered O'Brien, thumping down a plethoric sack by the side of Matthewson's. "Though it's little faith I'm having, John, that the beast can do the trick."

The Eldorado emptied its occupants into the street to see the test. The tables were deserted, and the dealers and game-keepers came forth to see the outcome of the wager and to lay odds. Several hundred men, furred and mittened, banked around the sled within easy distance. Matthewson's sled, loaded with a thousand pounds of flour, had been standing for a couple of hours, and in the intense cold (it was sixty below zero) the runners had frozen fast to the hard-packed snow. Men offered odds of two to one that Buck could not budge the sled. A quibble arose concerning the phrase "break out." O'Brien contended it was Thornton's privilege to knock the runners loose, leaving Buck to "break it out" from a dead standstill. Matthewson insisted that the phrase included breaking the runners from the frozen grip of the snow. A majority of the men who had witnessed the making of the bet decided in his favor, whereat the odds went up to three to one against Buck.

There were no takers. Not a man believed him capable of the feat. Thornton had been hurried into the wager, heavy with doubt; and now that he looked at the sled itself, the concrete fact, with the regular team of ten dogs curled up in the snow before it, the more impossible the task appeared. Matthewson waxed jubilant.

"Three to one!" he proclaimed. "I'll lay you another thousand at that figure, Thornton. What d'ye say?"

Thornton's doubt was strong in his face, but his fighting spirit was aroused—the fighting spirit that soars above odds, fails to recognize the impossible, and is deaf to all save the clamor for battle. He called Hans and Pete to him. Their sacks were slim, and with his own the three partners could rake together only two hundred dollars. In the ebb of their fortunes, this sum was their total capital; yet they laid it unhesitatingly against Matthewson's six hundred.

The team of ten dogs was unhitched, and Buck, with his own harness, was put into the sled. He had caught the contagion of the excitement, and he felt that in some way he must do a great thing for John Thornton. Murmurs of admiration at his splendid appearance went up. He was in perfect condition, without an ounce of superfluous flesh, and the one hundred and fifty pounds that he weighed were so many pounds of grit and virility. His furry coat shone with the sheen of silk. Down the neck and across the shoulders, his mane, in repose as it was, half bristled and seemed to lift with every movement, as though excess of vigor made each particular hair alive and active. The great breast and heavy fore legs were no more than in proportion with the rest of the body, where the muscles showed in tight rolls underneath the skin. Men felt these muscles and proclaimed them hard as iron, and the odds went down to two to one.

"Gad, sir! Gad, sir!" stuttered a member of the latest dynasty, a king of the Skookum Benches. "I offer you eight hundred for him, sir, before the test, sir; eight hundred just as he stands."

Thornton shook his head and stepped to Buck's side.

"You must stand off from him," Matthewson protested. "Free play and plenty of room."

The crowd fell silent; only could be heard the voices of the gamblers vainly offering two to one. Everybody acknowledged Buck a magnificent animal, but twenty fifty-pound sacks of flour bulked too large in their eyes for them to loose their pouch-strings.

Thornton knelt down by Buck's side. He took his head in his two hands and rested cheek on cheek. He did not playfully shake him, as was his wont, or murmur soft love curses; but he whispered in his ear. "As you love me, Buck. As you love me," was what he whispered. Buck whined with suppressed eagerness.

The crowd was watching curiously. The affair was growing mysterious. It seemed like a conjuration. As Thornton got to his feet, Buck seized his mittened hand between his jaws, pressing in with his teeth and releasing slowly, half-reluctantly. It was the answer, in terms, not of speech, but of love. Thornton stepped well back.

"Now, Buck," he said.

Buck tightened the traces, then slacked them for a matter of several inches. It was the way he had learned.

"Gee!" Thornton's voice rang out, sharp in the tense silence.

Buck swung to the right, ending the movement in a plunge that took up the slack and with a sudden jerk arrested his one hundred and fifty pounds. The load quivered, and from under the runners arose a crisp crackling.

"Haw!" Thornton commanded.

Buck duplicated the maneuver, this time to the left. The

crackling turned into a snapping, the sled pivoting and the runners slipping and grating several inches to the side. The sled was broken out. Men were holding their breaths, intensely unconscious of the fact.

"Now, MUSH!"

Thornton's command cracked out like a pistol-shot. Buck threw himself forward, tightening the traces with a jarring lunge. His whole body was gathered compactly together in the tremendous effort, the muscles writhing and knotting like live things under the silky fur. His great chest was low to the ground, his head forward and down, while his feet were flying like mad, the claws scarring the hard-packed snow in parallel grooves. The sled swayed and trembled, half-started forward. One of his feet slipped, and one man groaned aloud. Then the sled lurched ahead in what appeared a rapid succession of jerks, though it never really came to a dead stop again . . . half an inch . . . an inch . . . two inches. . . . The jerks perceptibly diminished; as the sled gained momentum, he caught them up, till it was moving steadily along.

Men gasped and began to breathe again, unaware that for a moment they had ceased to breathe. Thornton was running behind, encouraging Buck with short, cheery words. The distance had been measured off, and as he neared the pile of firewood which marked the end of the hundred yards, a cheer began to grow and grow, which burst into a roar as he passed the firewood and halted at command. Every man was tearing himself loose, even Matthewson. Hats and mittens were flying in the air. Men were shaking hands, it did not matter with whom, and bubbling over in a general incoherent babel.

But Thornton fell on his knees beside Buck. Head was against head, and he was shaking him back and forth. Those who hurried up heard him cursing Buck, and he cursed him long and fervently, and softly and lovingly.

"Gad, sir! Gad, sir!" spluttered the Skookum Bench king. "I'll give you a thousand for him, sir, a thousand, sir—twelve hundred, sir."

Thornton rose to his feet. His eyes were wet. The tears were streaming frankly down his cheeks. "Sir," he said to the Skookum Bench king, "No, sir. You can go to hell, sir. It's the best I can do for you, sir."

Buck seized Thornton's hand in his teeth. Thornton shook him back and forth. As though animated by a common impulse, the onlookers drew back to a respectful distance; nor were they again indiscreet enough to interrupt.

Etta Mae Johnson

GLORIA NAYLOR

Etta got out of the car unassisted and didn't bother to turn and watch the taillights as it pulled off down the deserted avenue adjacent to Brewster Place. She had asked him to leave her at the corner because there was no point in his having to make a U-turn in the dead-end street, and it was less than a hundred yards to her door. Moreland was relieved that she had made it easy for him, because it had been a long day and he was anxious to get home and go to sleep. But then, the whole business had gone pretty smoothly after they left the hotel. He hadn't even been called upon to use any of the excuses he had prepared for why it would be a while before he'd see her again. A slight frown crossed his forehead as he realized that she had seemed as eager to get away from him as he had been to leave. Well, he shrugged his shoulders and placated his dented ego, that's the nice part about these worldly women. They understand the temporary weakness of the flesh and don't make it out to be something bigger than it is. They can have a good time without pawing and hanging all onto a man. Maybe I should drop around sometime. He glanced into his rearview mirror and saw that Etta was still standing on the corner, looking straight ahead into Brewster. There was something about the slumped profile of her body, silhouetted against the dim street light, that caused him to press down on the accelerator.

Etta stood looking at the wall that closed off Brewster from the avenues farther north and found it hard to believe that it had been just this afternoon when she had seen it. It had looked so different then, with the August sun highlighting the browns and reds of the bricks and the young children bouncing their rubber balls against its side. Now it crouched there in the dim predawn light, like a pulsating mouth awaiting her arrival. She shook her head sharply to rid herself of the illusion, but an uncanny fear gripped her, and her legs felt like lead. If I walk into this street, she thought, I'll never come back. I'll never get out. Oh, dear God, I am so tired—so very tired.

Etta removed her hat and massaged her tight forehead. Then, giving a resigned sigh, she started slowly down the street. Had her neighbors been out on their front stoops, she could have passed through their milling clusters as anonymously as the night wind. They had seen her come down that street once in a broken Chevy that had about five hundred dollars' worth of contraband liquor in its trunk, and there was even the time she'd come home with a broken nose she'd gotten in some hair-raising escapade in St. Louis, but never had she walked among them with a broken spirit. This middle-aged woman in the wrinkled dress and wilted straw hat would have been a stranger to them.

When Etta got to the stoop, she noticed there was a light under the shade at Mattie's window, and she strained to hear what actually sounded like music coming from behind the screen. Mattie was playing her records! Etta stood very still, trying to decipher the broken air waves into intelligible sound, but she couldn't make out the words. She stopped straining when it suddenly came to her that it wasn't important what song it was—someone was waiting up for her. Someone who would deny fiercely that there had been any concern—just a little indigestion from them fried onions that kept me from sleeping. Thought I'd pass time by figuring out what you see in all this loose-life music.

Etta laughed softly to herself as she climbed the steps toward the light and the love and comfort that awaited her.

Dirge for Two Veterans

WALT WHITMAN

The last sunbeam
Lightly falls from the finish'd Sabbath,
On the pavement here, and there beyond it is looking,
Down a new-made double grave.

Lo, the moon ascending,
Up from the east the silvery round moon,
Beautiful over the house-tops, ghastly, phantom moon,
Immense and silent moon.

I see a sad procession,
And I hear the sound of coming full-key'd bugles,
All the channels of the city streets they're flooding,
As with voices and with tears.

I hear the great drums pounding,
And the small drums steady whirring,
And every blow of the great convulsive drums,
Strikes me through and through.
For the son is brought with the father,
(In the foremost ranks of the fierce assault they fell,
Two veterans son and father dropt together,
And the double grave awaits them.)

Now nearer blow the bugles,
And the drums strike more convulsive
And the daylight o'er the pavement quite has faded,
And the strong dead-march enwraps me.

In the eastern sky up-buoying,
The sorrowful vast phantom moves illumin'd,
('Tis some mother's large transparent face,
In heaven brighter growing.)

O strong dead-march you please me!
O moon immense with your silvery face you soothe me!
O my soldiers twain! O my veterans passing to burial!
What I have I also give you.

The moon gives you light,
And the bugles and the drums give you music,
And my heart, O my soldiers, my veterans,
My heart gives you love.

I Never Had It Made

JACKIE ROBINSON

Hate mail arrived daily, but it didn't bother me nearly as much as the threat mail. The threat mail included orders to me to get out of the game or be killed, threats to assault Rachel, to kidnap Jackie, Jr. Although none of the threats materialized, I was quite alarmed. [Branch] Rickey, early in May, decided to turn some of the letters over to the police.

That same spring the Benjamin Franklin Hotel in Philadelphia, where my teammates were quartered, refused to accommodate me. The Philadelphia Phillies heckled me a second time, mixing up race baiting with childish remarks and gestures that coincided with the threats that had been made. Some of those grown men sat in the dugout and pointed bats at me and made machine-gun like noises. It was an incredibly childish display of bad will.

I was helped over these crises by the courage and decency of a teammate who could easily have been my enemy rather than my friend. Pee Wee Reese, the successful Dodger short-stop, was one of the most highly respected players in the major leagues. When I first joined the club, I was aware that there might well be a real reluctance on Reese's part to accept me as a teammate. He was from Ekron, Kentucky. Furthermore, it had been rumored that I might take over Reese's position on the team. Mischief-makers seeking to create trouble between us had tried to agitate Reese into regarding me as a threat—a black one at that. But Reese, from the time I joined Brooklyn, had demon-strated a totally fair attitude.

Reese told a sportswriter, some months after I became a Dodger, "When I first met Robinson in spring training, I fig-ured, well, let me give this guy a chance. It may be he's just as good as I am. Frankly, I don't think I'd stand up under the kind of thing he's been subjected to as well as he has."

Reese's tolerant attitude of withholding judgment to see if I would make it was translated into positive support soon after we became teammates. In Boston during a period when the heckling pressure seemed unbearable, some of the Boston play-ers began to heckle Reese. They were riding him about being a Southerner and playing ball with a black man. Pee Wee didn't answer them. Without a glance in their direction, he left his position and walked over to me. He put his hand on my shoulder and began talking to me. His words weren't important. I don't even remember what he said. It was the gesture of comradeship and support that counted. As he stood talking with me with a friendly arm around my shoulder, he was saying loud and clear, "Yell. Heckle. Do anything you want. We came here to play baseball."

My Best Friend

HENRY MILLER

Believe it or not, it was my bike. This one I had bought at Madison Square Garden, at the end of a six-day race. It had been made in Chemnitz, Bohemia and the six-day rider who owned it was a German, I believe. What distinguished it from other racing bikes was that the upper bar slanted down towards the handle bars.

I had two other bikes of American manufacture. These I would lend my friends when in need. But the one from the Garden no one but myself rode. It was like a pet. And why not? Did it not see me through all my times of trouble and despair?

Yes, I was in the throes of love, a first love, than which nothing is more disastrous, as a rule. My friends had become disgusted with me; they were deserting me, or vice versa, one by one. I was desolate and alone. Whether my parents knew of my sad plight I don't recall, but I am sure they knew that something was bothering me. That "something" was a beautiful young woman named Una Gifford, whom I had met during my high school days.

As I have told elsewhere, we were such naïve creatures that perhaps we kissed two or three times—at a party, for example, never elsewhere. Though we both had telephones, we never telephoned one another. Why? I ask myself. (Because it would have been too bold perhaps.) We did write each other, but our letters were far apart. I remember how each day when I came home I turned first to the mantelpiece, where letters were kept, and it was almost always a blank absence that greeted me.

It was a period when I spent most of my days job-hunting (presumably). Actually, I went to a movie or the burlesk (if I could afford it). Suddenly I stopped doing this, and did nothing. Nothing but ride the bike. Often I was in the saddle, so to speak, from morning till evening. I rode everywhere and usually at a good clip. Some days, I encountered some of the six-day riders at the fountain in Prospect Park. They would permit me to set the pace for them along the smooth path that led from the Park to Coney Island.

I would visit old haunts, such as Bensonhurst, Ulmer Park, Sheepshead Bay and Coney Island. And always, no matter how diverse the scenery, I am thinking of her. Why doesn't she write me? When will the next party be? Etc., etc. I never had obscene thoughts about her, never dreamt of fucking her some day or even feeling her twat. No, she was like the princess in the fairy tale untouchable even in dream.

Nor did it ever occur to me to ride to Greenspoint, where she lived, and ride up and down her street in the hope of catching a glance of her. Instead I rode to the faraway places, scenes associated with my childhood—and happy days.

I thought of those idyllic days ruefully, with a heavy heart. Where were they now, these dear pals of my early youth? Were they going through the same anguish as I—or were some of them married already perhaps?

Sometimes, after having finished a good book, I would think of nothing but the characters in that book. The characters I speculated about most were usually out of Dostoevsky's novels, particularly *The Idiot*, *The Brothers Karamazov* and *The Possessed*. Indeed they were no longer characters from a book, but living creatures, people who haunted my reveries and dream life. Thus, thinking of some absurd individual like Smerdyakov I would suddenly burst out laughing, only to quickly check myself and veer my thoughts toward her. It was impossible to rid my mind of her. I was obsessed, fascinated, bereaved. If by some great chance I may have run into her I would doubtless have been tongue-tied.

Oh yes, once in a blue moon I would receive a letter from her, usually from some summer resort where she was spending her vacation. It would always be a short letter, couched in conventional language—and, to my mind, completely devoid of feeling. And my reply would pretty much match her letter despite the fact that my heart was breaking.

Heart break! There was a subject I gave myself to totally. Did other people my age suffer the same pangs? Was first love always as painful, awkward and barren as this? Was I perhaps a special case, a "romantic" of the first water? The answers to these self-addressed queries were generally written in my friends' faces. The moment I mentioned her name a look of total uninterest would emanate from them. "Still thinking about her?" "Haven't you had enough already0?" And so on. Implicit in their reactions was—how stupid can a guy become? And over a girl, no less.

As we spun along (me and my double) I went over these

fundamental facts backwards and forwards. It was like studying a theorem in algebra. And never once did I run into a com-
passionate soul! I became so desolate that I took to calling my
bike my friend. I carried on silent conversations with it. And of
course I paid it the best attention. Which meant that every time
I returned home I stood the bike upside down, searched for a
clean rag and polished the hubs and the spokes. Then I cleaned
the chain and greased it afresh. That operation left ugly stains
on the stone in the walkway. My Mother would complain, beg
me to put a newspaper under my wheel before starting to clean
it. Sometimes she would get so incensed that she would say to
me, in full sarcasm, "I'm surprised you don't take that thing to
bed with you!" And I would retort—"I would if I had a decent
room and a big enough bed."

That was another grievance I had to put up with—no room
of my own. I slept in a narrow hall bedroom, decorated only by
a shade to keep out the early morning light. If I read a book it
was at the dining room table. I never used the parlor except to
listen to phonograph records. It was when listening to some of
my favorite records (in the gloomy parlor) that I would go
through the greatest anguish about her. Each record I put on the

machine only deepened my sorrow. The individual who moved me the most—from ecstasy to absolute despair—was the Jewish Cantor Sirota. Next to him came Amato, the baritone at the Metropolitan Opera. And after these came Caruso and John McCormack, the beloved Irish tenor.

I took care of my wheel as one would look after a Rolls Royce. If it needed repairs I always brought it to the same shop on Myrtle Avenue run by a Negro named Ed Perry. He handled the bike with kid gloves, you might say. He would always see to it that neither front nor back wheel wobbled. Often he would do a job for me without pay, because, as he put it, he never saw a man so in love with his bike as I was.

There were streets I avoided and streets I favored. In some streets the setting or the architecture actually gave me a lift. There were sedate streets and run-down ones, streets full of charm and others horrendously dull. (Didn't Whitman say somewhere, "Architecture is what you do to it when you look at it"?) As a dromomaniac I was able to carry on an elaborate interior dialogue and at the same time be aware of the stage setting through which I was moving. Riding the bike was a little different; I had to watch my p's and q's or take a bad spill.

About this time the champion sprinter was Frank Kramer, whom of course I idolized. Once I managed to stay right behind him during one of his practice spins from Prospect Park to Coney Island. I remember him slapping me on the back when I caught up with him and, as he slapped my back, said, "Good work, young feller—keep it up!" That day was a red letter day in my life. For once I forgot about Una Gifford and gave myself up to dreams of riding in Madison Square Garden some day along with Walter Rutt, Eddie Root, Oscar Egg and the other celebrities of the track.

After a time, habituated to spending so many hours a day on my bike, I became less and less interested in my friends. My wheel had now become my one and only friend. I could rely on it, which is more than I could say about my buddies. It's too bad no one ever photographed me with my "friend." I would give anything now to know what we looked like.

Years later in Paris, I got myself another bike, but this one was an everyday sort, with brakes. To slow up demanded an effort on the part of one's legs. I could have had hand brakes put on my handle bars but that would have made me feel like a sissy. It was dangerous and thrilling to race through the city streets at top speed. Fortunately the automobile was not then much in evidence. What one really had to watch out for were young-sters playing in the middle of the street.

Mothers would warn their children to be careful, to keep their eyes open for that crazy young man who loves to speed through the streets. In other words I soon became a terror in the neighborhood.

I was both a terror and a delight. The kids were all begging their parents to get them a bike like mine.

How long can the heart ache without bursting? I have no idea. I only know that I put in a grueling period courting a girl in absentia. Even on my 21st birthday—a great event in my life—I sat some distance apart from her, too timid to open my mouth and tell her of my love. The last time I saw her was shortly after, when I plucked up the courage to ring her door-bell and tell her I was leaving for Juneau, Alaska, to become a placer miner.

It was almost harder to separate from my wheel from Chemnitz, Bohemia. I must have given it to one of my cronies, but to whom, I no longer remember.

It should be borne in mind that, although my heart was

breaking, I could still enjoy a good laugh. When I had the dough, I would often take in a vaudeville show at the Palace or spend the afternoon at the Houston Street Burlesk or some other burlesk house. The comedians from these shows were later to become figures in radio and television. In other words, I could literally laugh on the wrong side of my face. It was this ability to laugh in spite of everything that saved me. I had already known that famous line from Rabelais—"For all your ills I give you laughter." I can say from personal experience that it is a piece of the highest wisdom. There is so precious little of it today—it's no wonder the drug pushers and the psychoanalysts are in the saddle.

The Tent

RUMI

Outside, the freezing desert night.
This other night inside grows warn, kindling.
Let the landscape be covered with thorny crust.
We have a soft garden in here.
The continents blasted,
cities and little towns, everything
become a scorched, blackened ball.
The news we hear is full of grief for that future
but the real news inside here
is there's no news at all.

Friend, our closeness is this:
anywhere you put your foot, feel me
in the firmness under you.

How is it with this love,
I see your world and not you?

Listen to presences inside poems,
Let them take you where they will.

Follow those private hints,
and never leave the premises.

a time to learn

"My best friend is the one that brings out
the best in me."

—HENRY FORD

The Prophet

KAHLIL GIBRAN

And a youth said, Speak to us of Friendship.

And he answered, saying:

Your friend is your needs answered.

He is your field which you sow with love and reap with thanksgiving.

And he is your board and your fireside.

For you come to him with your hunger, and you seek him for peace.

When your friend speaks his mind you fear not the "nay" in your own mind, nor do you withhold the "ay."

And when he is silent your heart ceases not to listen to his heart;

For without words, in friendship, all thoughts, all desires, all expectations are born and shared, with joy that is unacclaimed.

When you part from your friend, you grieve not;

For that which you love most in him may be clearer in his absence, as the mountain to the climber is clearer from the plain.

And let there be no purpose in friendship save the deepening of the spirit.

For love that seeks aught but the disclosure of its own mystery is not love but a net cast forth: and only the unprofitable is caught.

And let your best be for your friend.

If he must know the ebb of your tide, let him know its flood also.

For what is your friend that you should seek him with hours to kill?

Seek him always with hours to live.

For it is his to fill your need, but not your emptiness.

And in the sweetness of friendship let there be laughter, and sharing of pleasures.

For in the dew of little things the heart finds its morning and is refreshed.

Friends for Life

SUSAN JONAS AND MARILYN NISSENSON

During the past few decades, questions have been raised among feminist psychologists about why mothers and daughters so often feel a special intimacy with each other, and whether it must of necessity always be reproduced. Elsewhere we have touched on the argument made by Nancy Chodorow and others that a special intimacy between women is the outgrowth of cultural assumptions about gender rather than the result of biological forces. In her book, *The Mother's Voice*, Dr. Kathy Weingarten takes this argument a step forward and challenges Chodorow, based on her own experience as a parent and clinician. Chodorow says that mothers perceive their sons as more different—more "other"—than their daughters. But Dr. Weingarten writes that the differences between herself and her firstborn son had no bearing on the degree of connection she felt toward him—that difference per se need not interfere with intimacy. In fact, she felt more closely connected to him from the moment of his birth onward than to anyone else in her life, including her second child, a daughter. As he grew, the fact of his gender, and the cultural demands that he—and she—dealt with it in certain prescribed ways, began to intrude. Her subsequent history with him has been an effort not to lose that early sense of connection. On the basis of her experience, Dr. Weingarten believes the cultural assumption that males lack the capacity to remain in connection can be negated if a mother works hard at understanding, and making herself understood by, her son.

This line of argument is provocative. It challenges mothers not to confuse sameness with closeness. It challenges them to try to stay in connection with sons. It challenges them to question the notion that they and their daughters will, a priori, be strongly connected, to focus instead on examining their relationship for what it is, and to search for ways in which they might make it better.

When we asked Angela A. how she would describe her relationship with Gretchen and Betsy, she said "warm" and "wonderful." These words recurred, along with "intense," "honest," "intimate," "empathetic," and the like, when we asked every woman we interviewed the same question. But the word that subsumed all these expressions of feeling, the word that was repeated most often was "friend."

Nellie Jenkins, mother of Natalie, twenty-one: "I think we're moving toward being friends. Before it was more a mother-daughter thing. Before I was more in charge. Now nobody needs to be."

Constance J., mother of Abby, thirty-two: "I think now we would consider ourselves more friends than mother and daughter. Now when she calls and asks my advice about something, she could just as well call a friend and ask the same question. I don't think she's calling me as an authority figure in her life, or that I know more than she does; it's more a sharing of the answer kind of thing. And it's the same for me. I ask her advice—but I could have asked another friend. I ask her because I respect Abby's opinion better than a friend's in some respects. I just don't think of her anymore as a daughter in the sense that I have any say in her life or any control over her life. And I don't want that. I think she's blossomed into her own woman, and maybe I can just be there to help her in some of her decisions through life."

Vivian Hedges, mother of Tina, thirty-one: "Absolutely it's

a friendship. But I don't call her to unload on her. It's 'Hello, sweetie, what are you doing?' Or 'Let's go shopping, we haven't gone to Loehmann's in a long time.' Not a heavy, analyzed kind of friendship."

Lorelle Phillips, mother of Sarah, thirty-three: "I think Sarah and I have a wonderful relationship. Nurturing. Close. Positive. And complex. The fact that we can have conflicts, and then resolve them, and go on from there—the fact that we're involved in each other's lives, that we can have a good time with one another—I can't imagine it being better."

Evelyn Tang, mother of Frances, thirty: "To me the high points are she and I sitting together just chatting, visiting, no big discussion, just sharing mutual things."

Helen Rucker, mother of Bridget Mary, thirty: "When she was in high school, I never liked it when people said, 'Oh, you're such good friends.' No. I was her mother. I could sit down and say, 'What are you doing about your college applications, or about the jobs you're supposed to do around the house?' which is the mother role. But it evolved into a friendship as she got older. Or certainly as she became sexually active. Or when she moved away from home."

"I think my daughters are the most important women in my life," says Letty Cottin Pogrebin. "I have friends, but if someone asked me, 'Who's the first person you would call to tell something important, or good, or bad,' it would be my husband, then my daughters, and my son. I must say I value the girls' opinions more than, or as much as, those of my female friends. I think they're very honest about why they're saying what they're saying. And they know me very well, they know my flaws a lot better than my friends do."

Honesty, acceptance, generosity, loyalty, and trust—these are all attributes of true friendship that Letty writes about in her book, *Among Friends*, in which she analyzed friendships among men, women, men and women, family members, co-workers, within racial and ethnic groups, and across cultural divides. We asked her why she didn't include mothers and their adult daughters in her pool. Equality is essential for friendship, Letty believes, and when she wrote the book her daughters were just eighteen—more her children than her equals. If she were writing today she would address the subject from firsthand experience. "How to be a friend and still be a parent is the issue with grown-up children," Letty feels. "If you're still in the control mode—if there's a power imbalance—then you're not friends."

A small group of the mothers we interviewed firmly believe that, as one of them put it, "a parent should remain parental." They may wish to perpetuate a subtle imbalance of power; they may want to retain the role of nurturer as exclusively their own. While they feel close to their daughters, they do not want an intimate, mutually reciprocal relationship. Says Paula S., mother of Maud, thirty-four, and Jessie, twenty-eight, "I don't think friendship is what I want. I think friendship involves a kind of intimacy, a sharing. I want serious boundaries that are respected. I like the generation gap. I want the generation gap. I think it's healthier for everybody. I always want to be the mother. I don't want to be a pal to my kids."

Sylvia Karchmar says of Lara, twenty-eight, and Dorian, twenty-five, "I've always wanted them to know that I am someone they can come to with whatever is on their minds, but I don't want them to think that I'm their girlfriend. I want to keep my credibility as their mother because you only have one mother. You can have lots and lots of friends, but a mother is a different level of relationship."

Martha R., mother of Emily, thirty, is also leery of mutuality. "I don't really embrace the notion of mothers and daughters being swell pals, that sort of thing. I mean, Emily and I are close—we depend on each other—but I'm still very much the mother. I guess I still believe there are certain things you don't need to share with your children. I want to protect her. I don't want her to feel alarmed. I don't want her to feel burdened. I don't want her to feel she has a mother she has to worry about."

Nancy Washington, mother of Linda, thirty-two, and Laura, twenty-eight, said, "I would not call us friends. I never wanted people to took at the three of us and say, 'Are you sisters?' I don't think that's a compliment. I say firmly, 'I am their mother.' I always felt that I want to be someone like my Aunt Jean, someone who is very comforting."

Comforting, protecting, nurturing are words that don't seem incompatible with friendship. We all value friends to whom we have turned for consolation and care when we have been in need, and whom we have in turn nurtured during stressful episodes in their lives. Friends understand and accept imbalances of need and control if they are temporary, but the long-term survival of a friendship depends upon an overriding equality in which need and nurture flow in both directions. The mothers who don't want to be friends want to preserve the role of caregiver or authority figure for themselves. They put less value on the reciprocal intimacy that makes true friendship possible.

And, as we have said, they were in a minority.

Most of the women we spoke to were pleased by the growing equality between themselves and their daughters. They were relieved to have moved beyond the caretaking mode. And yet—a mother's long history as the comforter, the nurturer, the caregiver cannot easily be ignored or abandoned. The reciprocity of need and nurture that characterizes other friendships can probably never exist between parent and adult child because the mother retains vestiges of her maternal role. Lucy Rose Fischer has studied the relationships between adult daughters and their mothers from the daughters' perspective. In her book, *Linked Lives*, Fischer states that "most mothers and daughters are both close and distant, and most are both peerlike and parental at the same time." Because of patterns inherent in the family structure, she believes, genuine peerlike friendships are somewhat uncommon and often somewhat cool in their nature, while relationships in which "mutual mothering" prevails are more common and more intimate. By mutual mothering, she means that each woman responds to the needs of the other, alternately nurturing and allowing herself to be cared for as the situation demands. Because mothers have the long history of being the nurturer, they probably continue in that role more than the daughter does, but there is enough give and take to make both women comfortable.

Mothers who are happy to call their relationship a friendship recognize this as a conundrum they are willing to live with. As Alice Van Tuyl, mother of Sarah, thirty-two, and Elizabeth, twenty-nine, says, "Friends is only one aspect of our relationship—we are also more than friends. You can never just be a friend to your daughter unless you have had nothing to do with her growing up and have just arrived when she's twenty-one. I don't think you can ever be just a friend. It's an inadequate word to describe the relationship. Behind the friend is always the parent. And you don't entirely abandon or abdicate that. Your worry level is always there. You don't have that for a friend no matter how close. You don't think, Gosh, I hope they're driving carefully tonight. I know they went to Boston for the weekend. And you're glad when the phone rings and they're home. Even your best friend doesn't call you when she gets home."

To a Friend

MATTHEW ARNOLD

Who prop, thou ask'st in these bad days, my mind?—
He much, the old man, who, clearest-souled of men,
Saw The Wide Prospect, and the Asian Fen,
And Tmolus hill, and Smyrna bay, though blind.

Much he, whose friendship I not long since won,
That halting slave, who in Nicopolis
Taught Arrian, when Vespasian's brutal son
Cleared Rome of what most shamed him. But be his

My special thanks, whose even-balanced soul,
From first youth tested up to extreme old age,
Business could not make dull, nor passion wild;

Who saw life steadily, and saw it whole;
The mellow glory of the Attic stage,
Singer of sweet Colonus, and its child.

Isabel

SARK

I first saw her in Big Sur, in the patio of a cliffside restaurant. She was sailing through, wearing wildly painted leather shoes, a very bright white blouse, and her white hair swept elegantly on top of her head.

I said to myself, "There's my new friend!" Then, I was struck by shyness and couldn't get up to meet her. An hour later, I saw her in the parking lot, getting into a big car with her women friends. I knew then that I had to meet her—and rushed over to give her a copy of my poster "How to Be an Artist."

She beamed at me, stopped and read the poster out loud, in its entirety, in her New Zealand accent.

She then said, "Why don't you give me a call in Berkeley, Dear!"

When I first visited her, she flung the door open, looked intently at me and said, "My Dear. Come in and lie down immediately! You look very nappish."

She brought me out to her marvelous garden, and I laid down on a brightly colored mat in the sun.

She then brought me succulent bits of food on tiny plates. I said to her, "Isabel, may I ask you a personal question?"

"Well yes, I hope it is personal!"

"Were you ever married?"

She replied impishly, "No, I escaped that particular thing."

Isabel owned a sportswear design company and had her own factory for 22 years. She traveled in "High Society" and had famous mentors. Yet, she doesn't speak of herself very much or often—you must be patient to find things out about her. She is consistently curious about other people and their stories.

Her home reflects her taste and style and is filled with flowers, bright colors, fabulous artwork, and simplicity.

Isabel is one of the wisest souls and youngest spirits I know. Once on a trip together, I found her on the balcony outside our room, with a flower in her hand, peering intently down. I asked her what she was doing.

"I'm looking into the hearts of flowers with this magnifying glass. Come see!"

Her approach to life is one of "Fresh Mind" and alive choices. Isabel gulps life.

She is also rather mysterious and quite reserved. She says she was raised by the "last of the Victorians."

Isabel can so graciously decline an invitation, you don't even realize for awhile that she's said no!

One time, I rented a house on top of a mountain in Big Sur for my 39th birthday, and invited Isabel for brunch. During the night, the rains had washed the roads out, and people coming to the party were digging their cars out of muddy ditches by the side of the road. People were also calling to say that they would-n't be coming due to the weather. All of a sudden, there was Isabel, who had driven her 1968 Plymouth Fury right up that washed out mountain road! She swept in with a big smile and basket of fresh muffins.

To Isabel, everything is brand new and the world is a wonder. Once my friend Brigette was in a car with Isabel and suddenly Isabel called out, "Oh look! Succulents!" Brigette thought she was talking about succulence, but Isabel had leapt out of the car to greet the succulent green plants she had spot-ted from the car window.

The Old Man and the Sea

ERNEST HEMINGWAY

He was an old man who fished alone in a skiff in the Gulf Stream and he had gone eighty-four days now without taking a fish. In the first forty days a boy had been with him. But after forty days without a fish the boy's parents had told him that the old man was now definitely and finally salao, which is the worst form of unlucky, and the boy had gone at their orders in another boat which caught three good fish the first week. It made the boy sad to see the old man come in each day with his skiff empty and he always went down to help him carry either the coiled lines or the gaff and harpoon and the sail that was furled around the mast. The sail was patched with flour sacks and, furled, it looked like the flag of perma-nent defeat.

The old man was thin and gaunt with deep wrinkles in the back of his neck. The brown blotches of the benevolent skin cancer the sun brings from its reflection on the tropic sea were on his cheeks. The blotches ran well down the sides of his face and his hands had the deep-creased scars from handling heavy fish on the cords. But none of these scars were fresh. They were as old as erosions in a fishless desert.

Everything about him was old except his eyes and they were the same color as the sea and were cheerful and undefeated.

"Santiago," the boy said to him as they climbed the bank from where the skiff was hauled up. "I could go with you again. We've made some money."

The old man had taught the boy to fish and the boy loved him.

"No," the old man said. "You're with a lucky boat. Stay with them."

"But remember how you went eighty-seven days without fish and then we caught big ones every day for three weeks."

"I remember," the old man said. "I know you did not leave me because you doubted."

"It was papa made me leave. I am a boy and I must obey him."

"I know," the old man said. "It is quite normal."

"He hasn't much faith."

"No," the old man said. "But we have. Haven't we?"

"Yes," the boy said. "Can I offer you a beer on the Terrace and then we'll take the stuff home."

"Why not?" the old man said. "Between fishermen."

They sat on the Terrace and many of the fishermen made fun of the old man and he was not angry. Others, of the older fishermen, looked at him and were sad. But they did not show it and they spoke politely about the current and the depths they had drifted their lines at and the steady good weather and of what they had seen. The successful fishermen of that day were already in and had butchered their marlin out and carried them laid full length across two planks, with two men staggering at the end of each plank, to the fish house where they waited for the ice truck to carry them to the market in Havana. Those who had caught sharks had taken them to the shark factory on the other side of the cove where they were hoisted on a block and tackle, their livers removed, their fins cut off and their hides skinned out and their flesh cut into strips for salting.

When the wind was in the east a smell came across the harbor from the shark factory; but today there was only the faint edge of the odor because the wind had backed into the north and then dropped off and it was pleasant and sunny on the Terrace.

"Santiago," the boy said.

"Yes," the old man said. He was holding his glass and thinking of many years ago.

"Can I go out to get sardines for you for tomorrow?"

"No. Go and play baseball. I can still row and Rogelio will throw the net."

"I would like to go. If I cannot fish with you, I would like to serve in some way."

"You bought me a beer," the old man said. "You are already a man."

"How old was I when you first took me in a boat?"

"Five and you nearly were killed when I brought the fish in too green and he nearly tore the boat to pieces. Can you remember?"

"I can remember the tail slapping and banging and the thwart breaking and the noise of the clubbing. I can remember you throwing me into the bow where the wet coiled lines were and feeling the whole boat shiver and the noise of you clubbing him like chopping a tree down and the sweet blood smell all over me."

"Can you really remember that or did I just tell it to you?"

"I remember everything from when we first went together."

The old man looked at him with his sun-burned, confident loving eyes.

"If you were my boy I'd take you out and gamble," he said. "But you are your father's and your mother's and you are in a lucky boat."

"May I get the sardines? I know where I can get four baits too."

"I have mine left from today. I put them in salt in the box."

"Let me get four fresh ones."

"One," the old man said. His hope and his confidence had never gone. But now they were freshening as when the breeze rises.

"Two," the boy said.

"Two," the old man agreed. "You didn't steal them?"

"I would," the boy said. "But I bought these."

"Thank you," the old man said. He was too simple to wonder when he had attained humility. But he knew he had attained it and he knew it was not disgraceful and it carried no loss of true pride.

"Tomorrow is going to be a good day with this current," he said.

"Where are you going?" the boy asked.

"Far out to come in when the wind shifts. I want to be out before it is light."

"I'll try to get him to work far out," the boy said. "Then if you hook something truly big we can come to your aid."

"He does not like to work too far out."

"No," the boy said. "But I will see something that he cannot see such as a bird working and get him to come out after dolphin."

"Are his eyes that bad?"

"He is almost blind."

"It is strange," the old man said. "He never went turtle-ing. That is what kills the eyes."

"But you went turtle-ing for years off the Mosquito Coast and your eyes are good."

"I am a strange old man."

"But are you strong enough now for a truly big fish?"

"I think so. And there are many tricks."

together forever

"With every friend who has been taken into the brown bosom
of the earth a part of me has been buried there. . . ."

—ARISTOTLE

The Funeral

AMY TAN

Kwan disappeared two months ago. I don't say "died," because I haven't yet allowed myself to think that's what happened.

I sit in my kitchen, eating granola, staring at the pictures of missing kids on the back of the milk carton. "Reward for any information," it reads. I know what the mothers of those children feel. Until proven otherwise, you have to believe they're somewhere. You have to see them once more before it's time to say good-bye. You can't let those you love leave you behind in this world without making them promise they'll wait.

I think Kwan intended to show me the world is not a place but the vastness of the soul. And the soul is nothing more than love, limitless, endless, all that moves us toward knowing what is true. I once thought love was supposed to be nothing but bliss. I now know it is also worry and grief, hope and trust, and believing in ghosts—that's believing that love never dies. If people we love die, then they are lost only to our ordinary senses. If we remember, we can find them anytime with our hundred secret senses. "This is a secret," I can still hear Kwan whispering. "Don't tell anyone. Promise, Libby-ah."

Siddhartha

HERMANN HESSE

When he reached the ferry, the boat was already there and the ferryman who had once taken the young Samana across, stood in the boat. Siddhartha recognized him. He had also aged very much.

"Will you take me across?" he asked.

The ferryman, astonished to see such a distinguished-looking man alone and on foot, took him into the boat and set off.

"You have chosen a splendid life," said Siddhartha. "It must be fine to live near this river and sail on it every day."

The rower smiled, swaying gently.

"It is fine, sir, as you say, but is not every life, every work fine?"

"Maybe, but I envy you yours."

"Oh, you would soon lose your taste for it. It is not for people in fine clothes."

Siddhartha laughed. "I have already been judged by my clothes today and regarded with suspicion. Will you accept these clothes from me, which I find a nuisance? For I must tell you that I have no money to pay you for taking me across the river."

"The gentleman is joking," laughed the ferryman.

"I am not joking, my friend. You once previously took me across this river without payment, so please do it today also and take my clothes instead."

"And will the gentleman continue without clothes?"

"I should prefer not to go further. I should prefer it if you would give me some old clothes and keep me here as your assistant, or rather your apprentice, for I must learn how to handle the boat."

The ferryman looked keenly at the stranger for a long time.

"I recognize you," he said finally. "You once slept in my hut. It is a long time ago, maybe more than twenty years ago. I took you across the river and we parted good friends. Were you not a Samana? I cannot remember your name."

"My name is Siddhartha and I was Samana when you last saw me."

"You are welcome, Siddhartha. My name is Vasudeva. I hope you will be my guest today and also sleep in my hut, and tell me where you have come from and why you are so tired of your fine clothes."

They had reached the middle of the river and Vasudeva rowed more strongly because of the current. He rowed calmly, with strong arms, watching the end of the boat. Siddhartha sat and watched him and remembered how once, in those last Samana days, he had felt affection for this man. He gratefully accepted Vasudeva's invitation. When they reached the river bank, he helped him to secure the boat. Then Vasudeva led him into the hut, offered him bread and water, which Siddhartha ate with enjoyment, as well as the mango fruit which Vasudeva offered him.

Later, when the sun was beginning to set, they sat on a tree trunk by the river and Siddhartha told him about his origin and his life and how he had seen him today after that hour of despair. The story lasted late into the night.

Vasudeva listened with great attention; he heard all about his origin and childhood, about his studies, his seekings, his pleasures and needs. It was one of the ferryman's greatest virtues that, like few people, he knew how to listen. Without his saying a word, the speaker felt that Vasudeva took in every word, quietly, expectantly, that he missed nothing. He did not await anything with impatience and gave neither praise nor blame—he only listened. Siddhartha felt how wonderful it was to have such a listener who could be absorbed in another person's life, his strivings, his sorrows.

However, towards the end of Siddhartha's story, when he told him about the tree by the river and his deep despair, about the holy Om, and how after his sleep he felt such a love for the river, the ferryman listened with doubled attention, completely absorbed, his eyes closed.

When Siddhartha had finished and there was a long pause, Vasudeva said: "It is as I thought; the river has spoken to you. It is friendly towards you, too; it speaks to you. That is good, very good. Stay with me, Siddhartha, my friend. I once had a wife, her bed was at the side of mine, but she died long ago. I have lived alone for a long time. Come and live with me; there is room and food for both of us."

"I thank you," said Siddhartha, "I thank you and accept. I also thank you, Vasudeva, for listening so well. There are few people who know how to listen and I have not met anybody who can do so like you. I will learn from you in this respect."

"You will learn it," said Vasudeva, "but not from me. The river has taught me to listen; you will learn from it, too. The river knows everything; one can learn everything from it. You have already learned from the river that it is good to strive downwards, to sink, to seek the depths. The rich and distinguished Siddhartha will become a rower; Siddhartha the learned Brahmin will become a ferryman. You have also learned this from the river. You will learn the other thing, too."

After a long pause, Siddhartha said: "What other thing, Vasudeva?"

Vasudeva rose. "It has grown later," he said, "let us go to bed. I cannot tell you what the other thing is, my friend. You will find out, perhaps you already know. I am not a learned man; I do not know how to talk or think. I only know how to listen and be devout; otherwise I have learned nothing. If I could talk and teach, I would perhaps be a teacher, but as it is I am only a ferryman and it is my task to take people across this river. I have taken thousands of people across and to all of them my river has been nothing but a hindrance on their journey. They have travelled for money and business, to weddings and on pilgrimages; the river has been in their way and the ferry-man was there to take them quickly across the obstacle. However, amongst the thousands there have been a few, four or five, to whom the river was not an obstacle. They have heard its voice and listened to it, and the river has become holy to them, as it has to me. Let us now go to bed, Siddhartha."

Siddhartha stayed with the ferryman and learned how to look after the boat, and when there was nothing to do at the ferry, he worked in the rice field with Vasudeva, gathered wood, and picked fruit from the banana trees. He learned how to make oars, how to improve the boat and to make baskets. He was pleased with everything that he did and learned and the days and months passed quickly. But he learned more from the river than Vasudeva could teach him. He learned from it continually. Above all, he learned from it how to listen, to listen with a still heart, with a waiting, open soul, without passion, without desire, without judgment, without opinions.

He lived happily with Vasudeva and occasionally they exchanged words, few and long-considered words. Vasudeva was no friend of words. Siddhartha was rarely successful in moving him to speak.

He once asked him, "Have you also learned that secret from the river; that there is no such thing as time?"

A bright smile spread over Vasudeva's face.

"Yes, Siddhartha," he said. "Is this what you mean? That the river is everywhere at the same time, at the source and at the mouth, at the waterfall, at the ferry, at the current, in the ocean and in the mountains, everywhere, and that the present only exists for it, not the shadow of the past, nor the shadow of the future?"

"That is it," said Siddhartha, "and when I learned that, I reviewed my life and it was also a river, and Siddhartha the boy, Siddhartha the mature man and Siddhartha the old man, were only separated by shadows, not through reality. Siddhartha's previous lives were also not in the past, and his death and his return to Brahma are not in the future. Nothing was, nothing will be, everything has reality and presence."

Siddhartha spoke with delight. This discovery had made

him very happy. Was then not all sorrow in time, all self-torment and fear in time? Were not all difficulties and evil in the world conquered as soon as one conquered time, as soon as one dispelled time? He had spoken with delight, but Vasudeva just smiled radiantly at him and nodded his agreement. He stroked Siddhartha's shoulder and returned to his work.

And once again when the river swelled during the rainy season and roared loudly, Siddhartha said: "Is it not true, my friend, that the river has very many voices? Has it not the voice of a king, of a warrior, of a bull, of a night bird, of a pregnant woman and a sighing man, and a thousand other voices?"

"It is so," nodded Vasudeva, "the voices of all living creatures are in its voice."

"And do you know," continued Siddhartha, "what word it pronounces when one is successful in hearing all its ten thousand voices at one time?"

Vasudeva laughed joyously; he bent towards Siddhartha and whispered the holy Om in his ear. And this was just what Siddhartha had heard.

As time went on his smile began to resemble the ferryman's, was almost equally radiant, almost equally full of happiness, equally lighting up through a thousand little wrinkles, equally childish, equally senile. Many travellers, when seeing both ferrymen together, took them for brothers. Often they sat together in the evening on the tree trunk by the river. They both listened silently to the water, which to them was not just water, but the voice of life, the voice of Being, of perpetual Becoming. And it sometimes happened that while listening to the river, they both thought the same thoughts, perhaps of a conversation of the previous day, or about one of the travellers whose fate and circumstances occupied their minds, or death, or their childhood; and when the river told them something good at the same moment, they looked at each other, both thinking the same thought, both happy at the same answer to the same question.

Two Women in Particular

ZORA NEALE HURSTON

Two women, among the number whom I have known inti-
mately, force me to keep them well in mind. Both of them have
rare talents, are drenched in human gravy, and both of them have
meant a great deal to me in friendship and inward experience.
One, Fannie Hurst, because she is so young for her years, and
Ethel Waters because she is both so old and so young for hers.

Understand me, their ages have nothing to do with their
birthdays. Ethel Waters is still a young woman. Fannie Hurst is
far from old.

In my undergraduate days I was secretary to Fannie Hurst.
From day to day she amazed me with her moods. Immediately
before and after a very serious moment you could just see her
playing with her dolls. You never knew where her impishness
would break out again.

One day, for instance, I caught her playing at keeping
house with company coming to see her. She told me not to
leave the office. If the doorbell rang, Clara, her cook, was to
answer it. Then she went downstairs and told Clara that I was

to answer the doorbell. Then she went on to another part of the house. Presently I heard the bell, and it just happened that I was on my way downstairs to get a drink of water. I wondered why Clara did not go to the door. What was my amazement to see Miss Hurst herself open the door and come in, greet herself graciously and invite herself to have some tea. Which she did. She went into that huge duplex studio and had toasted English muffins and played she had company with her for an hour or more. Then she came on back up to her office and went to work.

I knew that she was an only child. She did not even have cousins to play with. She was born to wealth. With the help of images, I could see that lonely child in a big house making up her own games. Being of artistic bent, I could see her making up characters to play with. Naturally she had to talk for her characters, or they would not say what she wanted them to. Most children play at that at times. I had done that extensively so I knew what she was doing when I saw her with the door half open, ringing her own doorbell and inviting herself to have some tea and muffins. When she was tired of her game, she just quit and was a grown woman again.

She likes for me to drive her, and we have made several tours. Her impishness broke out once on the road. She told me to have the car all serviced and ready for next morning. We were going up to Belgrade Lakes in Maine to pay Elizabeth Marbury a visit.

So soon next day we were on the road. She was Fannie Hurst, the famous author as far as Saratoga Springs. As we drove into the heart of town, she turned to me and said, "Zora, the water here at Saratoga is marvelous. Have you ever had any of it?"

"No, Miss Hurst, I never did."

"Then we must stop and let you have a drink. It would never do for you to miss having a drink of Saratoga water."

We parked near the famous United States Hotel and got out.

"It would be nice to stop over here for the night," she said. "I'll go see about the hotel. There is a fountain over there in the park. Be sure and get yourself a drink! You can take Lummox for a run while you get your water."

I took Lummox out of the car. To say I took Lummox for a run would be merely making a speech-figure. Lummox weighed about three pounds, and with his short legs, when he thought that he was running he was just jumping up and down in the same place. But anyway, I took him along to get the water. It was so-so as far as the taste went.

When I got back to the car, she was waiting for me. It was too early in the season for the hotel to be open. Too bad! She knew I would have enjoyed it so much. Well, I really ought to have some pleasure. Had I ever seen Niagara Falls?

"No, Miss Hurst. I always wanted to see it, but I never had a chance."

"Zora! You mean to tell me that you have never seen Niagara Falls?"

"No." I felt right sheepish about it when she put it that way.

"Oh, you must see the Falls. Get in the car and let's go. You must see those Falls right now." The way she sounded, my whole life was bare up to then and wrecked for the future unless I saw Niagara Falls.

The next afternoon around five o'clock, we were at Niagara Falls. It had been a lovely trip across Northern New York State.

"Here we are, now, Zora. Hurry up and take a good look at the Falls. I brought you all the way over here so that you could see them."

She didn't need to urge me. I leaned on the rail and looked and looked. It was worth the trip, all right. It was just like watching the Atlantic Ocean jump off Pike's Peak.

In ten minutes or so, Miss Hurst touched me and I turned around.

"Zora, have you ever been across the International Bridge? I think you ought to see the Falls from the Canadian side. Come on, so you can see it from over there. It would be too bad for you to come all the way over here to see it and not see it from the Bridge."

So we drove across the Bridge. A Canadian Customs Official tackled us immediately. The car had to be registered. How long did we intend to stay?

"You'd better register it for two weeks," Miss Hurst answered and it was done. The sun was almost down.

"Look, Zora, Hamilton is only a short distance. I know you want to see it. Come on, let's drive on, and spend the night at Hamilton."

We drove on. I was surprised to see that everything in Canada looked so much like everything in the United States. It was deep twilight when we got into Hamilton.

"They tell me Kitchener is a most interesting little place, Zora. I know it would be fun to go on there and spend the night." So on to Kitchener we went.

Here was Fannie Hurst, a great artist and globe famous, behaving like a little girl, teasing her nurse to take her to the zoo, and having a fine time at it.

Well, we spent an exciting two weeks motoring over Ontario, seeing the countryside and eating at quaint but well-appointed inns. She was like a child at a circus. She was a runaway, with no responsibilities.

Fannie Hurst, the author, and the wife of Jacques

Danielson, was not with us again until we hit Westchester on the way home. Then she replaced Mrs. Hurst's little Fannie and began to discuss her next book with me and got very serious in her manner.

While Fannie Hurst brings a very level head to her dressing, she exults in her new things like any debutante. She knows exactly what goes with her very white skin, black hair and sloe eyes, and she wears it. I doubt if any woman on earth has gotten better effects than she has with black, white and red. Not only that, she knows how to parade it when she gets it on. She will never be jailed for uglying up a town.

I am due to have this friendship with Ethel Waters, because I worked for it.

She came to me across the footlights. Not the artist alone, but the person, and I wanted to know her very much. I was too timid to go backstage and haunt her, so I wrote her letters and she just plain ignored me. But I kept right on. I sensed a great humanness and depth about her; I wanted to know someone like that.

Then Carl Van Vechten gave a dinner for me. A great many celebrities were there, including Sinclair Lewis, Dwight Fiske, Anna May Wong, Blanche Knopf, an Italian soprano, and my old friend, Jane Belo. Carl whispered to me that Ethel Waters was coming in later. He was fond of her himself and he knew I wanted to know her better, so he had persuaded her to come. Carl is given to doing nice things like that.

We got to talking, Ethel and I, and got on very well. Then I found that what I suspected was true. Ethel Waters is a very shy person. It had not been her intention to ignore me. She felt that I belonged to another world and had no need of her. She thought that I had been merely curious. She laughed at her error and said, "And here you were just like me all the time." She got warm and friendly, and we went on from there. When she was implored to sing, she asked me first what I wanted to hear. It was "Stormy Weather," of course, and she did it beautifully.

Then I did something for her. She told us that she was going to appear with Hall Johnson's Choir at Carnegie Hall, and planned to do some spirituals. Immediately, the Italian soprano and others present advised her not to do it. The argument was that Marian Anderson, Roland Hayes and Paul Robeson had sung them so successfully that her audience would make comparisons and Ethel would suffer by it. I saw the hurt in Ethel's face and jumped in. I objected that Ethel was not going to do any concertized versions of spirituals. She had never rubbed any hair off her head against any college walls and she was not going to sing that way. She was going to sing those spirituals just the way her humble mother had sung them to her.

She turned to me with a warm, grateful smile on her face, and said, "Thank you."

When she got ready to leave, she got her wraps and said, "Come on, Zora. Let's go on uptown." I went along with her, her husband, and faithful Lashley, a young woman spiritual singer from somewhere in Mississippi, whom Ethel has taken under her wing.

We kept up with each other after that, and I got to know her very well. We exchanged confidences that really mean something to both of us. I am her friend, and her tongue is in my mouth. I can speak her sentiments for her, though Ethel Waters can do very well indeed in speaking for herself. She has a homely philosophy that reaches all corners of Life, and she has words to fit when she speaks.

She is one of the strangest bundles of people that I have ever met. You can just see the different folks wrapped up in her if you associate with her long. Just like watching an open fire— the color and shape of her personality is never the same twice. She has extraordinary talents which her lack of formal education prevents her from displaying. She never had a chance to go beyond the third grade in school. A terrible fear is in me that the world will never really know her. You have seen her and heard her on the stage, but so little of her capabilities are seen. Her struggle for adequate expression throws her into moods at times. She said to me Christmas Day of 1941, "You have the advantage of me, Zora. I can only show what is on the stage. You can write a different kind of book each time."

She is a Catholic, and deeply religious. She plays a good game of bridge, but no card-playing at her house on Sundays. No more than her mother would have had in her house. Nobody is going to dance and cut capers around her on the Sabbath, either. What she sings about and acts out on the stage, has nothing to do with her private life.

Her background is most humble. She does not mind saying that she was born in the slums of Philadelphia in an atmosphere that smacked of the rural South. She neither drinks nor smokes and is always chasing me into a far corner of the room when I light a cigarette. She thanks God that I don't drink.

Her religious bent shows in unexpected ways. For instance, we were discussing her work in "Cabin in the Sky." She said, "When we started to rehearse the spirituals, some of those no-manners people started to swinging 'em, and get smart. I told 'em they better not play with God's music like that. I told 'em if I caught any of 'em at it, I'd knock 'em clean over into that orchestra pit." Her eyes flashed fire as she told me about it. Then she calmed down and laughed. "Of course, you know, Zora, God didn't want me to knock 'em over. That was an idea of mine."

And this fact of her background has a great deal to do with her approach to people. She is shy and you must convince her that she is really wanted before she will open up her tender parts and show you. Even in her career, I am persuaded that Ethel Waters does not know that she has arrived. For that reason, she is grateful for any show of love or appreciation. People to whom she has given her love and trust have exploited it heartlessly, like hogs under an acorn tree —guzzling and grabbing with their ears hanging over their eyes, and never looking up to see the high tree that the acorns fell from.

She went on the stage at thirteen and says that she got eight dollars a week for her first salary. She was so frightened that she had to be pushed on to sing her song, and then another member of the cast had to come on with her until she could get started. Then too, they had to place a chair for her to lean on to overcome her nervousness.

At fifteen, she introduced the "St. Louis Blues" to the world. She saw a sheet of the music, had it played for her, then wrote to W. C. Handy for permission to use it. Handy answered on a postal card and told her to go as far as she liked, or words to that effect. If W. C. Handy had only known at that time the importance of his act!

She is gay and somber by turns. I have listened to her telling a story and noticed her change of mood in mid-story. I have asked her to repeat something particularly pungent that she has said, and had her tell me, "I couldn't say it now. My thoughts are different. Sometime when I am thinking that same way, I'll tell it to you again."

The similes and metaphors just drip off of her lips. One day I sat in her living-room on Hobart Street in Los Angeles, deep in thought. I had really forgotten that others were present. She nudged Archie Savage and pointed at me. "Salvation looking at the temple forlorn," she commented and laughed. "What you doing, Zora? Pasturing in your mind?"

"It's nice to be talking things over with you, Zora," she told me another time. "Conversation is the ceremony of companionship."

Speaking of a man we both know, she said, "The bigger lie he tells, the more guts he tells it with."

"That man's jaws are loaded with big words, but he never says a thing," she said speaking of a mutual friend. "He got his words out of a book. I got mine out of life."

"She shot him lightly and he died politely," she commented after reading in the *Los Angeles Examiner* about a woman killing her lover.

Commenting on a man who had used coarse language, she said, "I'd rather him to talk differently, but you can't hold him responsible, Zora, they are all the words he's got."

Ethel Waters has known great success and terrible personal tragedy, so she knows that no one can have everything.

"Don't care how good the music is, Zora, you can't dance on every set."

I am grateful for the friendship of Fannie Hurst and Ethel Waters. But how does one speak of honest gratitude? Who can know the outer ranges of friendship? I am tempted to say that no one can live without it. It seems to me that trying to live without friends is like milking a bear to get cream for your morning coffee. It is a whole lot of trouble, and then not worth much after you get it.

In Memoriam M.K.H.

SEAMUS HEANEY

When all the others were away at Mass
I was all hers as we peeled potatoes.
They broke the silence, let fall one by one
Like solder weeping off the soldering iron:
Cold comforts set between us, things to share
Gleaming in a bucket of clean water.
And again let fall. Little pleasant splashes
From each other's work would bring us to our senses.

So while the parish priest at her bedside
Went hammer and tongs at the prayers for the dying
And some were responding and some crying
I remembered her head bent towards my head,
Her breath in mine, our fluent dipping knives—
Never closer the whole rest of our lives.

Delia Elena San Marco

JORGE LUIS BORGES

We said good-bye on one of the corners of the Plaza del Once.

From the sidewalk on the other side of the street I turned and looked back; you had turned, and you waved good-bye.

A river of vehicles and people ran between us; it was five o'clock on no particular afternoon. How was I to know that that river was the sad Acheron, which no one may cross twice?

Then we lost sight of each other, and a year later you were dead.

And now I search out that memory and gaze at it and think that it was false, that under the trivial farewell there lay an infinite separation.

Last night I did not go out after dinner. To try to understand these things, I reread the last lesson that Plato put in his teacher's mouth. I read that the soul can flee when the flesh dies.

And now I am not sure whether the truth lies in the ominous later interpretation or in the innocent farewell.

Because if the soul doesn't die, we are right to lay no stress on our good-byes.

To say good-bye is to deny separation; it is to say *Today we play at going our own ways, but we'll see each other tomorrow*. Men invented farewells because they somehow knew themselves to be immortal, even while seeing themselves as contingent and ephemeral.

One day we will pick up this uncertain conversation again, Delia—on the bank of what river?—and we will ask ourselves whether we were once, in a city that vanished into the plains, Borges and Delia.

about the authors

English poet and critic **MATTHEW ARNOLD**'s books include *Poems: A New Edition* (1853-4) and *New Poems* (1867). While a professor at Oxford he also published several critical works, including *Culture and Anarchy* (1869).

JORGE LUIS BORGES, born in Buenos Aires, is an internationally renowned cult writer famous for blurring reality and the fantastic. *Ficciónes* (1944) and *El Hacedor* (1960) are among his more well-known works.

SANDRA CISNEROS, noted author of *The House on Mango Street* and *Woman Hollering Creek and Other Stories*, is the recipient of two NEA fellowships for poetry and fiction, and the 1991 Lannan Literary Award.

Southern writer **FANNIE FLAGG** is also an actress, screenwriter, director, and comedienne. Her second novel, *Fried Green Tomatoes at the Whistle Stop Cafe*, was a bestseller and a feature film.

Poet, artist, and philosopher **KAHLIL GIBRAN** is the author of several works, most notably *The Prophet*, an illustrated inspirational classic celebrated worldwide for its poetic and mystical content.

SEAMUS HEANEY's collections include *Door Into the Dark* (1969) and *Selected Poems 1966-1987*. He has taught at Harvard and Oxford and won the 1995 Nobel Prize for Literature. He lives in Dublin.

A former "Lost Generation" writer of the 1920s expatriate community in Paris, **ERNEST HEMINGWAY** wrote such distinctive works as *A Farewell to Arms* and *The Old Man and the Sea*. He won the Nobel Prize for Literature in 1954.

In his writing, **HERMANN HESSE** masterfully blends spiritual, psychological, and philosophical traditions, as seen in the classics *Siddhartha* (1922) and *Steppenwolf* (1927). He won the Nobel Prize for Literature in 1946.

Harlem Renaissance writer **ZORA NEALE HURSTON**'s background in anthropology and folklore plays a major role in her work. *Mules and Men* and *Their Eyes Were Watching God* are among her best-known works.

SUSAN JONAS is the co-author of *Friends for Life*, a book about the bonds between mothers and daughters. She is the editor of many books and a former photography editor for *Discover* and *Time* magazines.

LISA JONES, author of *Bulletproof Diva: Tales of Race, Sex, and Hair*, has created plays for radio and stage and written three books with filmmaker Spike Lee. She lives in Brooklyn, New York.

JOHN KNOWLES has published several novels, a travel book, and a collection of stories. His celebrated *A Separate Peace* is a coming-of-age story generated from Knowles' student days at Phillips Exeter Academy.

ANNE LAMOTT injects humor and honesty into her fiction and nonfiction. Her books include *Bird by Bird: Some Instructions on Life and Writing*, *Operating Instructions: A Journal of My Son's First Year*, and *Rosie*.

JACK LONDON's prolific fiction and nonfiction often draws from his work experience on waterfronts, ships, and gold mining in the Yukon Territory. *Call of the Wild* and *White Fang* are two of his masterpieces.

HENRY MILLER's glory years began in Paris in the 1930s after years of struggling as a writer. One of his major works, *Tropic of Cancer* (1934), was the first of three books to be banned for its sexually explicit content.

GLORIA NAYLOR's storytelling won her the 1983 American Book Award for First Fiction for *The Women of Brewster Place*. She is also the author of *Mama Day*, *Bailey's Cafe*, and *Linden Hills*.

MARILYN NISSENSON was a writer and producer for CBS, NBC, and PBS before co-authoring *Friends for Life*, a book documenting mother-daughter relationships. She lives in New York City.

JACKIE ROBINSON was the first African-American to play baseball in the major leagues. Playing for the Brooklyn Dodgers, he endured a constant barrage of racial prejudice to become a 10-time all-star and Hall of Famer.

Religious scholar **JELALUDDIN RUMI** lived from 1207-1273 in Persia. His frequently quoted Sufi mystic prose has an almost eerie relevance in today's world. *The Essential Rumi* is a popular collection of poems.

SARK is an artist and best-selling author whose message has touched fans worldwide with her colorful and daring books. She lives in San Francisco with her cat Jupiter.

AMY TAN's stories reveal the intertwining and complex lives of her primarily Chinese and Chinese-American characters. Her books include *The Hundred Secret Senses*, *The Joy Luck Club* (also a feature film), and two books for children.

Poet and writer **WALT WHITMAN** (1819-1892) is perhaps best known for his masterful collection of poems, *Leaves of Grass*. Originally it was a commercial failure, deemed much too radical and scandalous for the times.

permissions & acknowledgments

Borges excerpt from "Delia Elena San Marco" from *Collected Fictions* by Jorge Luis Borges. ©1998 by María Kodama; translation ©1998 by Penguin Putnam Inc. Used by permission of Viking Penguin, a division of Penguin Putnam.

Cisneros excerpt from "My Lucy Friend Who Smells Like Corn" from *Woman Hollering Creek* by Sandra Cisneros ©1992 by Sandra Cisneros. Reprinted by permission of Susan Bergholz Literary Services.

Flagg excerpt from *Fried Green Tomatoes at the Whistle Stop Cafe* by Fannie Flagg. ©1987 by Fannie Flag. Reprinted by permission of Random House, Inc.

Heaney excerpt from "Clearances" from *Opened Ground: Selected Poems 1966-1996* by Seamus Heaney. ©1998 by Seamus Heaney. Reprinted by permission of Farrar, Straus & Giroux, Inc.

Hemingway excerpt from *The Old Man and the Sea* by Ernest Hemingway. ©1952 by Ernest Hemingway. Renewed ©1980 by Mary Hemingway. Reprinted by permission of Scribner, a division of Simon & Schuster, Inc.

Hesse excerpt from *Siddhartha* by Hermann Hesse. ©1951 by New Directions Publishing Corp. Reprinted by permission of New Directions Publishing Corp.

Hurston excerpt from chapter XIII "Two Women in Particular" from *Dust Tracks on a Road* by Zora Neale Hurston. ©1942 by Zora Neale Hurston. Renewed ©1970 by John C. Hurston. Reprinted by permission of HarperCollins Publishers, Inc.

Jonas excerpt from *Friends for Life* by Susan Jonas and Marilyn Nissenson. ©1997 by Susan Jonas and Marilyn Nissenson. Reprinted by permission of William Morrow & Company, Inc.

Jones excerpt from *Bulletproof Diva* by Lisa Jones. ©1994 by Lisa Jones. Reprinted by permission of Doubleday, a division of Random House, Inc.

Knowles excerpt from *A Separate Peace* by John Knowles. ©1959 by John Knowles. Reprinted by permission of Curtis Brown, Ltd.

Lamott excerpt from *Rosie* by Anne Lamott. ©1983 by Anne Lamott. Used by permission of Viking Penguin, a division of Penguin Putnam Inc.

Miller excerpt from *My Bike & Other Friends* by Henry Miller. ©1978 by Henry Miller. Reprinted by permission of Capra Press.